The Life of

Alexander Fleming

Judith Kaye

Twenty-First Century Books

A Division of Henry Holt and Company

New York

PHOTO CREDITS
page 4: Library of Congress. page 20: St. Mary's Hospital Medical
School. page 25: Wellcome Institute Library, London. page 39: St.
Mary's Hospital Medical School. page 46: © Dr. Jeremy Burgess,
Science Source/Photo Researchers. page 66: Imperial War Museum.
page 74: The Hulton Picture Company.

Twenty-First Century Books
A Division of Henry Holt and Company, Inc.
115 West 18th Street
New York, NY 10011

Henry Holt® and colophon are registered trademarks of
Henry Holt and Company, Inc.
Publishers since 1866.

Library of Congress Cataloging-in-Publication Data

Kaye, Judith
The Life of Alexander Fleming / Judith Kaye. — 1st ed.
p. cm. — (Pioneers in Health and Medicine)
Includes bibliographical references and index.
Summary: Presents the life of the Nobel Prize-winning British
bacteriologist whose discovery of penicillin in 1928 revolutionized
the treatment of disease.
1. Fleming, Alexander, 1881-1955—Juvenile literature. 2.
Bacteriologists—Great Britain—Biography—Juvenile literature.
[1. Fleming, Alexander, 1881-1955. 2. Scientists. 3.
Penicillin—History.]
I. Title. II. Series.
QR31.F5K38 1993
589.9'009'2—dc20 [B] 92-34420 CIP AC

ISBN 0-8050-2300-3
First Edition—1993

Printed in Mexico
All first editions are printed on acid-free paper ∞.

10 9 8 7 6 5 4 3 2 1

Contents

Alexander Fleming in 1955

1

The Funny Blue Mold

On a September afternoon in 1928, a rather short man stood at his laboratory bench at St. Mary's Hospital in London. Dr. Alexander Fleming's blue eyes were fixed on the flat, round glass dish in his hand. A researcher, Dr. Fleming grew disease-causing bacteria—plants so tiny that a single one cannot be seen without the aid of a microscope—in dishes like this one. After peering closely at the petri dish for a long moment, Fleming turned to a co-worker who stood beside him. "That's funny," Fleming observed.

Years later, Fleming described what was funny about what he had seen in the petri dish. A furry blue mold, like the fuzzy molds that grow on old bread or spoiled foods, had started to grow in the dish. Molds are simple plants without leaves, stems, or roots. Molds cannot produce their own food. Instead, they get their food from the material on which they grow. Many molds reproduce by producing tiny spores. These microscopic spores, which can develop into molds, constantly drift through the air, settling here, there, and everywhere. Fleming, like other experimenters, had often found mold spores growing in the gelatin-like substance, called agar, in which he grew his bacteria.

But this particular mold was unusual. In the petri dish in which it was growing, there were no bacteria left near the blue substance. As Fleming explained, "On this particular occasion, the mould [mold] which developed appeared to be dissolving the bacteria. That was very unusual, so instead of casting out the contaminated culture with appropriate language, I made some investigations and the more I investigated it the more interesting it became."

When he saw that the mold seemed to be dissolving the bacteria, Fleming calmly but quickly took careful steps to preserve the mold. Then, he eagerly began testing the unusual substance. Fleming's tests showed that the mold was not poisonous. His investigations also indicated that the mold seemed to prevent the growth of some kinds of harmful bacteria, bacteria that can lead to serious illness, or even death.

When he found that the mold seemed to prevent the growth of harmful bacteria, Dr. Fleming became excited. He began to wonder whether the mold could be used to cure people of illnesses caused by bacteria.

Although few of his fellow researchers at St. Mary's Hospital shared Fleming's enthusiasm for studying the blue substance, he worked with the mold for several months. Dr. Fleming's research came to an end before he was able to develop a way for the mold to be used safely and effectively in treating people. It was not until years later that Fleming, and the world, realized the full importance of his discovery. The funny blue mold was penicillin—a drug that would one day be considered the most useful medicine in the world.

Other scientists, most notably Sir Howard Florey and Dr. Ernst Chain, would later develop the blue mold discovered by Fleming into the penicillin that became the miracle drug we know today. But we remember Fleming because it was he who first recognized the possible importance of the blue mold. It was Fleming who took the crucial step of preserving the mold so it could be studied by other doctors. And it was Fleming who performed the early tests that later convinced other scientists to pursue the development of penicillin.

When asked, Fleming would modestly say that his discovery of penicillin was a matter of chance, or fortune. After all, the mold had accidentally landed and grown in his petri dish. However, as he pointed out just a few years before his death, "Fortune will greatly influence the distribution of prizes in this world but we must not merely wait for fortune to smile on us. We must prepare ourselves with the knowledge which will enable us to take advantage of the good things which fortune puts on our plate." The fact that Fleming didn't throw out the blue mold when he saw it, showed that his mind was prepared to recognize the potential value of what fortune sent his way.

How did Fleming know to preserve and test the

penicillin mold, rather than discarding it? What had prepared him to recognize the possible significance of the funny blue mold?

The preparation of Fleming's mind began when he was still a child. He developed the ability to observe the tiniest changes in nature early, by exploring the Scottish countryside around his home. His schooling in Scotland, and later in London, taught Alexander how to draw his own conclusions about facts presented to him. Later, during World War I, young Doctor Fleming worked in a French hospital. There, he saw daily that many lives were lost to infections caused by bacteria. Still later, while working with bacteria in his London research laboratory, Fleming learned to recognize and test unusual findings.

Yet, these experiences, as valuable as they were, would have counted for nothing if Alexander Fleming's mind had not also been prepared with a thorough knowledge of the history of medicine.

Fleming knew that for most of human history, people had had no real understanding of what disease was, what caused it, or how it spread. For thousands of years, they had believed that illness was some sort of curse or a punishment sent by angry gods. People in some cultures practiced forms of witchcraft or religious rituals to try to cure a sick person. Others used parasites, such as leeches, to suck the "bad" blood from a patient.

Occasionally, these methods seemed to work. But, really, there was little anyone could do to cure or prevent illness. Once a contagious disease, capable of being spread from person to person, took hold in a population, it often continued to spread until large numbers of people were affected. One such disease swept across Europe in the fourteenth century, killing one quarter of the population in just three years!

In 1796, an important discovery alerted scientists to the possibility that disease might be prevented. An English country doctor named Edward Jenner discovered how to protect people from catching smallpox, an often deadly disease. Jenner found that people who were exposed first to cowpox—a related, though much less serious, illness—were usually able to avoid catching smallpox.

After Jenner's discovery, more progress was made toward understanding disease. Scientists learned that germs, or microbes, organisms too small to be seen with the naked eye, were often the source of infection. But scientists knew very little about germs. They did not know how germs were created, or how they multiplied. Most scientists guessed that germs were created spontaneously, out of nonliving matter.

Then, during the second half of the nineteenth century, the French chemist Louis Pasteur made an astonishing discovery—germs come from other germs. Pasteur reasoned that the spread of germs could be stopped, if germs could be killed or kept from multiplying.

Pasteur's discovery that germs multiply changed the direction of medical research. Scientists now began looking for ways to fight germs in order to prevent illnesses.

In 1874, Joseph Lister, a surgeon in Scotland, studied Pasteur's work on germs and made another important medical discovery: how to control germs during operations. In the late nineteenth century, many patients survived operations only to die later of infections caused by microbes that had entered their open wounds. Lister began to use antiseptics, which check the action of germs, to clean surgical tools and bandages. His methods helped save thousands of lives.

Another important step in understanding germs was taken in 1876 by Robert Koch, a German researcher. Koch identified the microbe that caused anthrax, a disease common among sheep and cattle, which could spread to people. Koch became the first scientist to link a specific germ to a specific disease.

In France, Louis Pasteur studied Koch's work. He published reports of how germs carry contagious diseases, diseases that are spread by contact. Then, using the work that Jenner had done with cowpox and smallpox as a base, Pasteur went on to develop vaccines. A vaccine is made from dead or weakened germs of a disease. When injected into a person, a vaccine helps protect the person against catching the disease.

So, at the time Alexander Fleming first saw the blue mold, the art of medical healing was already at a turning point. The spread of germs had been sharply reduced through the adoption of sanitary, or hygienic, practices. Inoculation with vaccines, as a method of preventing future illnesses, was catching hold. Bacteriologists in laboratories around the world were racing to identify the germs that caused specific diseases and working to produce vaccines to prevent those diseases. The laboratory in which Alexander Fleming worked was engaged in just such research.

Almost all scientists of Fleming's time already agreed on the importance of developing and using vaccines to protect a healthy person against catching diseases. They did not yet agree on the best methods of fighting germ-caused illnesses after they had already infected a person.

When Alexander Fleming noticed the blue mold that afternoon in 1928, he did not know that this mold would turn out to be the magic that cured people of many germ-caused illnesses after they were already ill. Fleming had no way of guessing that his funny mold would come to be considered the greatest discovery of twentieth-century medical science. He would probably have been very surprised to hear that the penicillin mold would prove so effective a bacteria-fighter that it extended the average lifespan of people throughout the world by more than thirty years!

2

A Career by Chance

Alexander Fleming was born on August 6, 1881, at Lochfield Farm, an isolated sheep farm near the town of Darvel in southwestern Scotland. Alexander was the seventh of eight children. He had two older stepbrothers, Hugh and Tom, and two older stepsisters, Jane, who died when Alexander was only two years old, and Mary. His father, Hugh Fleming, had married Alexander's mother, Grace Morton, when he was sixty. Grace gave birth to four more children: Grace, John, Alexander, who was called Alec by his family, and Robert.

The Fleming family was neither poor nor rich. Their farmhouse was larger than many. Yet it had only three bedrooms to serve Mr. and Mrs. Fleming, the adult children, four young children, and frequent visiting relatives. Like most houses in the late 1800s, the Flemings' home was heated by open fires. And the house had no indoor plumbing. The family washed in the kitchen sink with water carried by bucket from a nearby spring.

Despite the rough and crowded living conditions, as an adult Alexander declared, "I think I was fortunate in being brought up as a member of a large family on a remote farm. We had no money to spend, and there was nothing to spend money on. We had to make our own amusements, but that is easy in such surroundings." As the youngest children, John, Alec, and Robert, certainly had an easy time amusing themselves. The boys had no regular chores, although they sometimes helped with the animals. Usually, they were left free to roam the rolling Scottish countryside together, and they learned the location of every hill and creek by heart. The Flemings' sheep farm had over 800 acres for the boys to explore. But the brothers also wandered across neighboring farms, seeking blueberries and strawberries in season, collecting birds' eggs, hunting, and fishing.

Alec and Robert collected the eggs of peewits, members of a family of shore birds known as plovers, when they wanted some extra pocket money. Collecting these eggs is illegal in Scotland today, but, back then, a local grocer bought the eggs to sell to fancy restaurants in England.

Alec and his brothers were enthusiastic fishermen. Although the boys were not supposed to play games or sports on Sunday, Robert remembered that "Mother had a tolerant mind. To tell the truth we could do anything within reason so long as we did it . . . out of sight of the house and neighbors." One Sunday, Alec and Robert caught some beautiful trout. They could not bear to throw the fish back, so they decided to hide them near their house in a small pool of the stream. The following morning, Monday, the two brothers announced they were going fishing before breakfast. When they returned promptly with two fine trout for the table, Robert recalled, "Mother only smiled and said we had been clever and quick that morning but asked no questions. Hugh and John grinned broadly."

Mrs. Fleming was a warm and affectionate mother, who successfully united the children of two marriages into one family. She was lively and fun to be with, and she frequently interrupted her chores to play games with her children. Mr. Fleming, however, did not do as much with the children. An elderly man, he suffered a stroke when Alexander was quite young.

When Alexander turned five, his parents sent him to school. He soon learned that country living had disadvantages as well as advantages. He had to walk to school, no matter what the weather. Alec's first school was only a mile from home. But, when he was about ten, Alexander transferred to a larger school in Darvel, and his walk became four miles— each way. Before he journeyed out on cold days, Alec's mother gave him two freshly baked potatoes. The potatoes kept his hands warm in his pockets and later made up part of his lunch.

Twice daily, Alec trekked the same path. When the creeks ran high, he removed his shoes to cross them. When downpours or snowstorms made the going slow, he often arrived soaked to the skin. But, unless the road was made impassable by snowdrifts, Alec made the journey every school day. Because he enjoyed studying the nature around him, he never found the walks dull.

Alexander Fleming did not realize until he was an adult that, on these long walks, he "unconsciously learned a great deal about nature, much of which is missed by a towndweller." After he became a research scientist, Fleming pointed out that he developed his keen ability to observe small changes in nature during these long walks to school.

Education was a serious business to Alexander Fleming's family. Alec's father, who was already seventy when Alexander started school, worried about the future of his younger sons. Mr. Fleming knew that only Hugh, the eldest son, would be able to take over the family's sheep farm. (Traditionally, the oldest son inherited the family home and business.) The other Fleming boys would need good educations to prepare them for other professions. Alexander's sisters, Mary and Grace, were expected to marry and raise children, as was the custom in the late 1800s.

Even on his deathbed in October of 1888, Mr. Fleming worried about his younger sons. He asked Hugh and Tom, who was then a medical student, to help their stepbrothers get a good start in life, and both promised to do their best. Alexander was only seven when his father died.

A few years after Mr. Fleming's death, Tom moved to London, England, to open a medical practice specializing in eye care. Mary moved with him, to keep house. As soon as Tom's practice became established, both Hugh and Tom, realizing that the younger Flemings needed more educational and job opportunities than rural Scotland could offer, encouraged their stepbrothers to move to London as well.

One by one, the three youngest children moved in with Tom and Mary. John was fifteen when he went to London in 1893. Alec came next, in the summer of 1895, when he was not yet fourteen. And twelve-year-old Robert arrived in London six months later. The only Fleming son remaining on the farm was Hugh, who lived there until he died at the age of seventy-nine.

Roaming busy London the same way they had roamed the peaceful hills and valleys around the family sheep farm, Alec and Robert explored the city on foot. At that time, street traffic was powered by horses. Iron horseshoes clanked, and iron-covered wheels rattled, on the stone streets. Steam trains rumbled underground, shooting billows of steam through grates in the road. Porters pushing handcarts yelled warnings to pedestrians, and vendors shouted out what they were selling from their wagons. The boys found the bustle and noise of London very different from the quiet gurgling of the fast-running creeks at home.

In writing about his brother's life, Robert gave an account of exploring London with Alexander. "Those who knew Alec well knew he liked company, but he was anything but talkative. When going around either of us would draw each other's attention to anything interesting without much comment. He knew I would ask what I wanted and he would answer if he knew."

The Fleming home in London was crowded, but pleasant, with plenty of games and competitions in the evenings. According to Robert, Tom never let the boys become bored. "He would invent Geography competitions, History competitions and indeed any kind of competition even to working out the odds on something or other," Robert remembered.

The family unit in London changed a bit when Mary left to marry. Grace gladly took her sister's place as housekeeper. With Grace away, only Mrs. Fleming remained with Hugh at Lochfield Farm.

Alec and Robert took business classes at the Regent Street Polytechnic School in London. Schoolwork came easily to them. In fact, despite their rural schooling, both boys were at least two years ahead of the other students in their age groups. The boys' most difficult task seemed to be learning to minimize their strong Scottish accents, in order to fit in with their schoolmates.

Alexander passed all his courses with high marks, and finished school by the time he was sixteen. Then, because he needed money to support himself, he went to work as a clerk in a shipping office. He spent most of his time copying documents and preparing records of passengers and cargo. The work did not interest him at all. When the Boer War—a conflict between Britain and the Dutch settlers of South Africa—broke out in 1899, Alexander eagerly volunteered to join the army.

Along with John and Robert, Alec joined the London Scottish, an army regiment mostly made up of Scots living in London. The young men kept their regular jobs and trained with the regiment in the evenings and on weekends. This regiment turned out to be as much a social club as a military unit. The Flemings learned to swim, so that they could play water polo. Alec and Robert also joined in the rifle shooting matches and proved to be skilled marksmen.

Alec became especially popular with the other men in the regiment. Although he seldom spoke much, a habit from boyhood that remained with him throughout his life, he was friendly and seemed to be a good listener. In addition, he always participated enthusiastically in all games and activities. Although Alec, like his brothers, was never called upon to fight, he remained active in regimental social activities for most of his life.

When Alexander was twenty, he received a small inheritance from an uncle. John and Robert, who got similar legacies, planned to pool their money and open a business of their own. But Alexander, although eager to quit his job as a clerk, had no plans for his money. Finally, at Tom's suggestion, Alec decided to become a medical student—not because medicine particularly interested him, but because Tom was doing well as a doctor.

In 1901, Alexander easily passed the examinations needed for admission to a London medical school. Now that he was qualified to enter a school, he needed to decide where to study. Instead of making a purposeful decision and setting a course for himself, Alexander again seemed to go where chance led him. There were twelve medical schools in London at the time, he explained later. "I lived about equidistant from three of them. I had no knowledge of any of these three, but I had played water polo against St. Mary's, and so to St. Mary's I went." Fleming entered St. Mary's Hospital Medical School in October 1901, and remained connected with the hospital for fifty-four years, his entire professional life.

In medical school, Alec was always at or near the top of his class. During his first year, his high marks earned him a scholarship and two prizes that paid all of his tuition fees. As Robert later observed, "He had the exceptional gift of reading a text book and understanding all that mattered very quickly." Yet his family also noticed that Alexander did not spend much time studying. He continued to participate in the family games and competitions each evening. Robert described how Alec studied—when he did study. "When he read a medical book, he flipped through the pages very rapidly, and groaned out loud when he caught the author making a mistake. There was a great deal of groaning."

After he finished medical school in 1906, Alexander Fleming thought he would study surgery. He changed his plans, however, when Sir Almroth Wright asked him to be his assistant. One of Wright's responsibilities was to act as chief of the St. Mary's bacteriology laboratory, a department involved in the study of bacteria.

Fleming seated in the first row, right, at St. Mary's
Hospital Medical School

Wright did not invite Fleming to join his staff because of the young doctor's outstanding academic record. It seems that St. Mary's Hospital had a rifle team, a good one. While a medical student, Fleming had been among the team's best marksmen. One of Fleming's teammates was on Wright's staff. This doctor, worried that St. Mary's would lose the Inter-Hospitals Shooting Cup without Fleming, convinced Almroth Wright to hire Fleming as an assistant. Once again, chance—in this case, sports—had more to do with Alexander's career path than any seriously thought-out decision of his own.

Fleming once spoke to a group of medical students about the connection between team sports and the effective practice of medicine. "If a student gave up all games and spent all his time reading textbooks, he might know his books better than the next man," he admitted. However, Fleming continued, there was "far more in medicine than mere bookwork. You have to know men and you have to know human nature. There is no better way to learn about human nature than by indulging in sports, more especially team-sports." Therefore, he advised, "play games, and you will be able to read your books with a greater understanding of your patients, and that will make you better doctors."

And so, Alexander Fleming joined Sir Almroth Wright's lab as a research biologist, beginning a career that led to the most famous medical discovery of all time.

3

Playing with Microbes

When Alexander Fleming joined the Inoculation Department at St. Mary's Hospital in 1906, the department's laboratories were so cramped that Fleming could scarcely set up his equipment. But he soon learned to make room for each new experiment by arranging and rearranging his old materials.

The main goal of the Inoculation Department was to develop vaccines. Edward Jenner had created the first vaccine in 1796, more than one hundred years before Fleming began his work. Jenner, an English country doctor, noticed that dairymaids, who tended and milked cows, had clear, smooth complexions. Many other people in the late 1700s had deep scars on their faces. The scars remained after a person recovered from smallpox, a serious and often deadly disease.

When Jenner began to investigate, he discovered that dairymaids did not often get smallpox. Instead, they caught a related illness called cowpox. Cowpox was not nearly as serious, and it rarely left scars. Jenner began to think that cowpox somehow helped to protect the dairymaids against catching smallpox. He decided to expose other people to cowpox to see whether they, too, would be protected against smallpox after recovering from cowpox.

To test his theory, Jenner inoculated a healthy boy with cowpox by injecting a preparation made from the germs that cause cowpox through the skin into the boy's body. The boy developed cowpox. But, months later, when inoculated with smallpox, he did not develop that dreaded disease. Jenner was the first to use vaccination—the introduction of microorganisms of a disease into a person's body, in order to help the body build immunity, or resistance, against that disease or a related one.

Unfortunately, it took scientists about eighty years to fully benefit from Jenner's discovery. While working on a cure for anthrax, a disease affecting sheep and cattle, Louis Pasteur studied Jenner's work. Pasteur then created a mixture of dead and weakened anthrax germs, which he injected into healthy sheep and cattle. The animals became slightly sick. But later, when Pasteur injected the same animals with deadly live anthrax microbes, the animals remained healthy. They had built up an immunity to anthrax. Pasteur called the mixture he injected a "vaccine," in honor of Jenner. (In Latin, the word *vacca* means cow.)

The Inoculation Department at St. Mary's was continuing the work of Jenner and Pasteur, attempting to develop new vaccines that would build immunity against more and more diseases. As part of this work, Alexander Fleming examined hospital patients. He drew blood and collected tissue samples from those patients who had diseases that might be treatable with vaccines. The blood and tissue samples were used in developing vaccines that were then used to treat the patients.

Sir Almroth Wright, the head of the Inoculation Department, was an enthusiastic believer in vaccines. He himself had discovered a vaccine to protect against typhoid, a deadly disease spread by contaminated food, water, and milk. Wright was confident that vaccine therapy would someday be used to cure, as well as to prevent, disease. Wright's enthusiasms ruled the Inoculation Department, and his opinions and decisions were considered law. Wright was forty-five, twenty years Fleming's senior, when Fleming joined the department.

Fleming often listened quietly while Wright, who talked frequently and at length, described some elaborate project or plan. When Fleming softly responded, "Why?" or "It won't work, sir," Wright, as well as Alexander's co-workers, learned to listen. Many times, Fleming's judgment proved correct.

Despite the fact that Alexander Fleming did not often chat with other staff members, his easygoing manner soon made him as popular with his co-workers as with the members of his Scottish regiment. Fleming seldom smiled, but his actions proved that he was not always as serious as he looked. Once, two students asked Fleming to help them make some equipment from glass tubing. Fleming showed

Sir Almroth Wright

the students how to blow the glass properly, and how to soften and shape it over a flame. Then, warming bits of leftover glass, he shaped a glass cat and some glass mice from the pieces. Fleming had a large collection of little animals he had made from leftover glass.

According to his brother Robert, Alec Fleming never lost his childhood love of games and kept "something of the boy in him always." In fact, he seemed to become more and more attracted to games as he grew older, and he used his inventiveness to create amusements for himself, just as he had done as a boy. Once, for example, Alexander set up a miniature golf course through the rooms of a friend's house. Another time, he devised a way to play croquet at night, by lighting the hoops with candles. And, whenever he had some extra time at St. Mary's, Fleming pitched pennies on the rug squares in his office.

Even in the laboratory, Fleming invented ways to amuse himself. "You treat research like a game," Sir Almroth Wright once grumbled to Fleming. And, when Fleming was asked what he did for a living, he often answered, "I play with microbes."

One of Fleming's favorite games was growing germ pictures in his laboratory. To do this, Fleming first isolated strains of the microbes he knew would grow in the brightest colors. Next, he filled a petri dish with a growing medium, such as agar. Then, Fleming designed his picture, and sowed the germs into the prepared dish in careful patterns. Finally, he placed the dish in an incubator to keep the germs warm. In a day or so, the microbes erupted in bright colors, forming a miniature painting. Once, when the Queen of England visited the lab, Fleming supposedly prepared a germ picture of a Union Jack, the British flag. The Queen was reported not to have been at all amused by a representation of the national symbol in germs.

This game of Fleming's took great skill, care, and a thorough knowledge of which microbes grow in which substances, and at what temperatures. In order to create a successful picture, Fleming had to have solid scientific knowledge as well as creativity and ingenuity. These same qualities were evident in all the serious lab work he did at St. Mary's.

During his first few years at the Inoculation Department, Alec lived with John, Robert, and his mother, who had replaced Grace as the family housekeeper after Grace married. Fleming frequently involved his family in his microbe chasing. Whenever anyone was sick, he took germ samples back to the lab to prepare a vaccine. "I must have had my arm punctured and injected with hundreds of different kinds of dead microbes in those days," Robert remembered. Fortunately, "Alec was a master of technique. He could insert the needle of a syringe into you so that you hardly felt it."

Alexander Fleming became well known for his skill in administering injections. It was because of this skill that Almroth Wright assigned Fleming a job in 1910—a job that turned out to be of great importance to Fleming's future. The assignment was to inject a drug called salvarsan into patients suffering from syphilis. Syphilis is a sexually transmitted disease. In the early 1900s, it infected thousands of people every year. The disease can have terrible long-term effects, such as blindness and madness. And, if left untreated, syphilis often leads to death.

When a German doctor, Paul Ehrlich, made salvarsan from a combination of chemicals, the drug was hailed as a "magic bullet." Injected into a vein in the body, salvarsan seemed to aim straight for the syphilis germ and kill it, without doing any other harm. In the early 1900s, injecting directly into a vein, instead of into a muscle, was a new and difficult practice, and few doctors were skilled enough to do it. Fleming and a colleague published a paper about salvarsan in which they explained that injecting the drug into a vein "is much less painful, and enables the patient to get about with perfect comfort in much less time than the older method. Its effect is quicker and more certain, and recurrences are less common."

Fleming, who may have been the first doctor in England to administer salvarsan, quickly gained a reputation as the doctor to see when the first signs of syphilis appeared. The treatment with salvarsan became so popular that Fleming, whose salary from the Inoculation Department was not very large, opened a private practice to treat people infected with syphilis.

When the Inoculation Department first began treating patients with salvarsan, Fleming and Wright were not sure they trusted the treatment. Wright, especially, was suspicious of being able to use chemicals to kill germs. He preferred to prevent disease by using vaccines in order to build up the body's immunity. He still hoped to make a vaccine that would cure a diseased patient. But, when Wright saw first-hand the quick cures that followed treatment with salvarsan, he became convinced that salvarsan was one chemical that worked. He and Fleming became involved in a medical practice that was still fairly new: the introduction of an antibacterial medicine into a diseased body to fight germs.

The lab's work with salvarsan came to a sudden halt when Britain entered World War I in August, 1914. The Germans had just seized Belgium, as part of their plan to attack France—Britain's ally. Since the fighting was on the European continent, British soldiers and physicians were sent from England to France, to support allied troops there.

Wright immediately put his lab at the service of the war effort. He, Fleming, and a few other members of the Inoculation Department traveled to Boulogne, France, where they set up a makeshift research laboratory in the attic of a casino. The fancy rooms below had once been used for gambling. Now, they were wards for soldiers wounded on the battlefield, or ill with some disease caught in the trenches. The researchers' task was to study the soldiers' infected wounds and diseases. The researchers then advised other doctors on how best to treat the soldiers.

More than forty years earlier, when France was at war with Prussia, another researcher, Louis Pasteur, had done similar work, examining matter from the infected wounds of soldiers. Pasteur had found that the matter, or tissue, was swarming with microbes. He believed that the germs were spread by doctors who moved from one patient to another without washing their hands or their instruments. Once the microbes landed on a soldier's open wound, the germs multiplied. Pasteur urged the use of hygienic methods to decrease the spread of germs.

Joseph Lister, a Scottish surgeon, was impressed with Pasteur's findings. Lister looked for ways to promote hygiene in operating rooms. He took carbolic acid, a very poisonous acid, and made it weaker by diluting it. Then he washed his hands, instruments, and the bandages and dressings used on wounds, with the mild acid solution. Lister became the first doctor to use chemicals that check the action of germs to prevent infection. These chemicals are called antiseptics.

During the early part of World War I, many army surgeons were following the sanitary practices taught by Lister. Wounds were cut open, cleaned, and wrapped with bandages soaked in germ-killing antiseptic, just as Lister had recommended. Doctors also kept their operating rooms clean, and even sprayed the air with antiseptics.

Nevertheless, infections that occurred after operations remained a major problem. Many infections lasted weeks, even months. And, often, patients died from their infections.

World War I was the first war in which high explosives were used. Bombs dropped from military airplanes, and bullets fired from armored tanks and machine guns, produced wounds that were deep and riddled with shrapnel—fragments of metal. Wright and Fleming began to suspect that the antiseptics used by doctors were not reaching the germs hidden far inside the shrapnel-packed wounds. Because this idea was hard for other doctors to accept, Fleming devised a clever experiment to prove the theory.

Heating a glass tube, Fleming gently tugged at bits of the tube to form pointed, hollow spikes. These long and narrow spikes were a fairly good model of a wound created by explosives. In such a wound, germ-laden matter is driven deep into hidden pockets in the body. Next, Fleming poured germ-contaminated blood serum, the clear fluid that oozes from cuts and wounds, into the tube. After discarding the serum, he filled the tube with a strong antiseptic solution. He left the antiseptic in the tube overnight. In the morning, Fleming once again emptied the tube. This time he refilled it with fresh blood serum that was free of germs. Within a short time, however, microbes were again growing vigorously in the serum.

Fleming explained to other doctors that the antiseptic could not reach and kill the germs that had penetrated into the tiniest crevices in the glass tube. Likewise, antiseptics applied to the surface of a wound could not reach all the germs on a scrap of cloth or bit of metal that had been wedged deep into a wound. The germs survived and multiplied. As a result, they were able to invade the rest of the body again.

While experimenting with antiseptics, Fleming also became convinced that applying antiseptics could do more harm than good. He showed that, before fresh wounds were treated with antiseptics, the body's germ-fighting white blood cells were plentiful and actively fighting the microbes. After the antiseptics were applied, however, there were fewer white blood cells. The antiseptics that doctors used to kill the germs, Fleming reasoned, were also killing the white blood cells, and so were weakening the body's own defenses against infection. Fleming concluded that antiseptics were useful for keeping surface areas and equipment clean. But antiseptics were harmful if applied inside a wound.

Backed by Wright, Fleming advised surgeons to remove all dead tissue and foreign matter from a wound, and to clean it with a strong, germ-free salt solution. Such a cleaning would kill some germs. But it would not destroy the germ-fighting white blood cells, which Wright called "the best antiseptic." The cells would be able to continue battling the infection deep inside a wound. Then, Fleming recommended, surgeons should stitch up the wound and apply a sterile dressing to the surface.

Only some of the younger doctors were willing to follow this advice during the remainder of World War I. They proved that the treatment worked very well, if it was done quickly, before a serious infection developed. By the time World War II broke out, almost twenty-five years later, Fleming's method of treating wounds had become standard.

Fleming's experiences with infected wounds made him begin to question Wright's belief that all disease and infection would someday be controlled by the use of vaccines. Vaccines were certainly important. They could spare people the agony of catching an illness. But how should people who had already contracted an infection or a disease be treated? Was there a cure that could be injected into a diseased body, a cure that would attack the infection from within? Was there another magic bullet like salvarsan?

4

Crying in the Interest of Science

In 1919, Wright's research group returned to St. Mary's, after five years in France. Fleming, now thirty-eight years old, had good reason to be excited about coming home. Four years earlier, in December of 1915, he had married, while on leave from his war work. His wife, Sarah McElroy Fleming, was a lively, blond Irish woman. She was a trained nurse and had founded a nursing home in London.

Not much is known about Alexander's early romance with Sarah, who seemed, in many ways, to be Alexander's opposite. While he was even-tempered, she was quick to anger. While Alexander preferred listening, Sarah loved to talk. While he liked to relax, Sarah constantly busied herself with household or outdoor chores, from cleaning and cooking to gardening, to throwing parties for their friends. Fleming once said fondly of his wife, "She does all the work, and provides all the conversation."

When Alexander returned to England, Sarah sold her nursing home to devote herself to her husband and domestic life, which she loved. Fleming closed the private practice he had opened to treat people with syphilis, and he cut back on his laboratory hours. In London, the Flemings lived in an apartment near Alec's brother John, who had met and married Sarah's twin sister, Elizabeth. In 1921, Sarah and Alexander bought a vacation home in the peaceful countryside of Suffolk, in eastern England. The couple drove to their country retreat nearly every weekend, and they often invited friends and family members to join them. Everyone enjoyed fishing, boating, and swimming in a little river that wound through the property. Alec and Sarah built a tennis court and a croquet lawn lighted with candles for night play. The house came with three acres of neglected gardens, and both Flemings soon became devoted gardeners.

Perhaps the greatest sadness in Alexander's life during the early years of his marriage was the death, in 1922, of his beloved stepbrother Tom. It was Tom who had opened his home to the younger Flemings when Alec was a teenager, and who had encouraged him to study medicine.

A second, but this time happy, major event in Fleming's family life was the birth of a son in 1924, after Sarah and Alexander had been married nine years. The delighted parents named the little boy Robert, probably after Alexander's younger brother. A proud father, Fleming gave up many sports, including golf, to spend more time with his son.

But Fleming continued his involvement in the Scottish regiment's social activities, and, every afternoon after work, he visited a men's club where he had tea, played chess, pool, or cards, and had a drink, before going home for dinner. His best friend at the club was Vivian Pitchforth, an artist who was completely deaf. Fleming and Pitchforth were well-suited companions. Fleming didn't like to chat, and Pitchforth couldn't hear, so they could get right down to their game of pool without bothering about conversation.

In addition to spending time at his club and with his family, Fleming still spent many hours in the lab "playing" with microbes. Much of his laboratory work involved preparing cultures—cultivating microbes in much the same way as for his germ pictures—for the hospital.

Two years after his return from France, Fleming was promoted to Assistant Director of the Inoculation Department. He now shared a tiny laboratory with two other staff members. One of the researchers, Dr. V. D. Allison, was very neat. He recalled that: "Early on, Fleming began to tease me about my excessive tidiness in the laboratory. At the end of each day's work I cleaned my bench, put it in order for the next day and discarded tubes and culture plates for which I had no further use." It seemed that Fleming, for his part, kept his cultures for two or three weeks until, in Allison's words, "his bench was overcrowded with 40 or 50 cultures. He would then discard them, first of all looking at them individually to see whether anything interesting or unusual had developed."

One November evening in 1921, Fleming was examining his cultures as he cleaned up his clutter of petri dishes, basins, test tubes, and flasks. A particular culture dish caught his attention. He handed it to Dr. Allison with the comment, "This is interesting."

Allison later described the scene. "The plate [petri dish] was one on which he had cultured mucus from his nose some two weeks earlier." The plate, Allison remembered, "was covered with golden-yellow colonies of bacteria, obviously harmless contaminations deriving from the air or dust of the laboratory," which must have gotten onto the culture before Fleming covered the dish, or when he periodically uncovered it to check on the culture's progress. What was remarkable, Allison explained, "was that in the vicinity of the blob of nasal mucus there were no bacteria." Fleming and Allison concluded that, "something had diffused [spread out] from the nasal mucus to prevent the germs from growing."

With Allison's help, Fleming isolated the substance that had prevented the growth of germs near the mucus. Next, Fleming experimented with mucus from other people's noses to see whether the substance was common to everyone. Then, he tried other body fluids, such as saliva and tears. All of these fluids showed this lytic activity—an ability to dissolve the cells of the bacteria. The lytic activity was particularly strong in tears.

Fleming described one of his early tests on this natural antiseptic. "When I studied this new substance,

I put into a test-tube a thick, milky suspension of bacteria, added a drop of tear, and held the tube for a few seconds in the palm of my hand. The contents became perfectly clear. I had never seen anything like it."

When Sir Almroth Wright heard about Fleming's discovery, he named the new substance "lysozyme." (*Lyso* is a Greek word meaning to dissolve.) Wright also encouraged Fleming and Allison to continue their investigation of the substance. To carry out their research, Fleming and Allison needed a good supply of lysozyme. They placed drops of lemon juice into their eyes to encourage the flow of tears. They asked visitors to the laboratory to cry in the interest of science. The two scientists even paid laboratory assistants to produce tears for their experiments, and Fleming told one young asssistant with eyes red from crying, "If you cry often enough, you'll soon be able to retire!"

In December 1921, about a month after he discovered lysozyme, Fleming presented his findings to the Medical Research Club, a group of prestigious scientists who met to discuss ongoing research and suggest further areas of investigation. Unfortunately, Fleming was a poor lecturer. He spoke in a flat monotone, and so softly that he could scarcely be heard. As a result, he didn't communicate his own enthusiasm and hopes for the new substance to his audience. When Fleming finished his rather awkward presentation, nobody even asked a question about what Fleming hoped to do with the substance he had discovered.

Fleming did not let the reaction of the medical

Fleming in his laboratory at St. Mary's, 1925

society discourage him. For the next five years, he continued working with lysozyme, testing to see if this natural germ killer could be of use in fighting disease. In order to discover which bacteria were dissolved by lysozyme, Fleming used a "gutter plate." He cut a gutter, or little ditch, through the gelatin substance in the petri dish. He then filled the gutter with a mixture of agar and lysozyme. Next, he placed streaks of the various microbes that he wanted to test across the gutter. Germs that were destroyed by lysozyme would not grow in or near the lysozyme-filled gutter.

Fleming experimented with dozens of different microbes that cause serious disease. One after another, the microbes grew straight across the gutter, as if the lysozyme were not there. To Fleming's dismay, only harmless microbes seemed to be stopped by lysozyme.

We now know that lysozyme, a mild antiseptic, is probably part of the body's first-line defense against bacteria in areas, such as the eyes and nose, that are exposed to many airborne bacteria. In such areas, there is little blood flow, and therefore few bacteria-fighting white blood cells. Today, physicians use lysozyme to treat minor eye and intestinal infections.

Alexander Fleming, however, was interested in which harmful bacteria lysozyme would attack, and the answer was none. The substance apparently could not be used to fight disease. Naturally, Fleming was disappointed. But his experience with the testing of lysozyme served a more important function than the scientist could then have known. It prepared Fleming for his work on a much greater discovery— his greatest—the discovery of penicillin.

5

A Potential Germ Killer

Alexander Fleming finished testing lysozyme in 1926. His life had settled into a comfortable routine. He, Sarah, and Robert continued to spend holidays and weekends at their country home. In London, the family now rented a house in an attractive part of the city called Chelsea. The house was larger than their old apartment, and much closer to the club Fleming visited after work.

In the laboratory, Fleming cultured microbes for the hospital, oversaw the production of vaccines, trained younger researchers, and conducted research for Wright. But he also continued working on projects that interested him personally. And his interest in the possibility of finding systemic cures for diseases—cures that would affect the entire body after they were introduced into the body—remained strong.

Fleming's work in treating syphilis had taught

him the value of a cure that could be injected into the body. His experience during World War I had shown him that cures that would not harm disease-fighting white blood cells were desperately needed for both contagious diseases and deep-seated infections. And his efforts to discover whether lysozyme might be used to fight harmful microbes had taught him how to test a promising substance.

Now, Fleming needed a promising new substance to test. His discovery of that substance was due not only to his keen eye and his prepared mind, but also to the same laboratory clutter that had earlier led to the discovery of lysozyme. Late in his career, when Fleming was shown a clean, orderly lab in a giant chemical company, he commented, "I never could have discovered penicillin here. Everything is much too clean and tidy."

Fleming's workspace at St. Mary's was famous throughout the lab for its clutter and chaos. In September 1928, forty-seven-year-old Alexander Fleming returned from his summer vacation. He, Sarah, and four-year-old Robert had been relaxing at their country home, and now Fleming was setting up his lab bench for the work he would do that fall. Stacked on a corner of his worktable were piles of petri dishes he had used to prepare cultures before leaving on vacation. Fleming planned to wash these dishes in a pan of disinfectant. But, because he was such a careful observer, he was doing what he usually did before disinfecting his culture plates— carefully examining the culture in each petri dish, to be sure it was of no further interest, before tossing the dish into the disinfectant.

As Fleming examined and discarded cultures, another researcher came in to see him. The men chatted while Fleming continued to examine and discard dishes. "As soon as you uncover a culture dish something tiresome is sure to happen," Fleming reportedly told his colleague. "Things fall out of the air." Fleming knew from experience that, before a petri dish was covered, or anytime the cover was lifted, something could settle on a culture and contaminate it.

To illustrate his point, Fleming casually picked up a petri dish he had already examined and thrown aside. The plate had landed on a pile of dishes and hadn't yet come in contact with the disinfectant in the pan. Some staphylococcus germs, which cause boils and other skin infections, were growing in the culture.

As Fleming gazed at the dish a second time, something in it caught his attention. A blue mold was growing on the culture. This in itself was not surprising. Molds were growing on many of the petri dish cultures he was examining. Near this mold, however, Fleming saw something unusual. As he explained in 1945, to a *New York Times* reporter, "The bacteria around the spot of mold had apparently disappeared while those some distance from it had continued to increase." Between the spot where the bacteria had disappeared, and the spot where they were growing normally, was an area in which some microbes appeared to be dissolving.

Like lysozyme, the new mold in the petri dish

seemed to be a substance that checked or prevented bacterial growth. Unlike lysozyme, however, this substance was affecting the growth of a kind of bacteria that can cause serious infection.

What Fleming said to his co-worker at the moment he actually noticed the blue mold was merely "That's funny." The other researcher glanced at the culture, but was not very impressed with the blue mold. Fleming, however, was excited. During the rest of that day, he showed the petri dish to anyone who stopped in his lab. He carried the culture around with him to show to others in the Inoculation Department.

But Fleming had been excited before about one discovery or another. For years, he had showed off petri dishes in which lysozyme was destroying microbes. But lysozyme could not be used against harmful diseases. Now, no one seemed very interested in spending time on another lysozyme.

Fortunately, Alexander Fleming did not think that investigating the new blue mold was a waste of time. To keep evidence of the mold's bacteria-fighting power, he first photographed the petri dish. Then he fixed, or sterilized, some of the culture, stopping the growth of both the mold and the bacteria in it.

Next, Fleming took a little of the mold from the remainder of the culture and put it into a test tube filled with meat broth. The broth would preserve the mold, and the mold would continue to grow on top of the broth. As the mold grew, a thick, soft mass—first white, then green, then black—covered the surface.

Fleming called the broth in which he grew the

A magnification of the penicillin mold

mold "mold juice," and it was this mold juice that Fleming used to carry out his experiments. Eventually, Fleming discovered that the mold was a strain of penicillia, a fairly common group of molds found on ripening cheese, stale bread, and rotting fruit. The mold's name comes from the Latin word *penicillus*, meaning brush; under a microscope, the mold resembles tiny brushes. Fleming named the active ingredient in the mold juice "penicillin."

Fleming's lab notebook shows that he tested the penicillin mold from October 1928 until March 1929. Alexander knew from his work with lysozyme that a long series of tests must be performed to determine whether penicillin would be useful. First, the substance needed to be tested in many cultures, so that the reseacher could determine which bacteria would be affected by the penicillin.

Next, the substance needed to be tested on animals to see whether the drug would be safe, and whether it would effectively fight disease. When experimenting on animals, researchers first administer a drug to healthy animals to see if the drug causes any side effects. Then, the drug is administered to animals infected with a disease, to see whether or not the drug fights that disease. If the drug cures the animals without harming them, researchers perform the same tests on human beings.

Fleming knew that, even if penicillin proved effective in fighting diseases, there would be many other important questions to answer: How should penicillin be developed and prepared? How should it be administered—how often, how much, and in what strength? Would penicillin work if swallowed, and could it be swallowed safely? Would it work if injected, and could it be injected safely? Could it be applied to an open wound to prevent or fight infection?

Alexander Fleming began the long process of testing penicillin by first trying to identify which types of bacteria were affected by the drug. For these experiments, he used the same gutter-plate method he had used to test lysozyme. This time, Fleming filled the gutter with a mixture of agar and mold juice. Soon, he had evidence that penicillin stopped the growth of many harmful bacteria, including those that cause scarlet fever, pneumonia, meningitis, and diphtheria. These results excited Fleming. "It looks as though we have got a mold that can do something useful," he commented to a colleague.

As he continued testing the substance, Fleming realized that he needed another form of penicillin than that in the mold juice. The broth could not be injected into the body because the proteins in the mold juice could harm the body. And the juice lost its ability to slow or stop germ growth in a few days. Finally, it took days for penicillin to grow in the broth, and large quantities of broth yielded only small amounts of penicillin.

Not a chemist himself, Fleming asked two young co-workers, who although they were not chemists had some background in chemistry, to help him purify, concentrate, and stabilize penicillin. At the same time, Fleming began an investigation of other strains of mold, to see if he could find another antibacterial agent or a better source of penicillin than the blue mold. Thousands of different molds exist, and Fleming knew very little about them.

Fleming collected molds from any item on which molds would grow. However, only one mold, out of the many strains he tested, seemed to have any bacteria-fighting power, and that mold appeared to be identical to the original blue mold he had discovered.

Meanwhile, Fleming continued to check on the progress of his co-workers who were trying to develop a better form of penicillin. Unfortunately, the penicillin investigations were not a high priority in a laboratory that specialized in developing vaccines. The frustrated researchers made some progress, but not as much as Fleming had hoped.

Continuing to test the mold juice, Fleming soon discovered that, unlike the antiseptics used during World War I, penicillin did not slow or stop the work of white blood cells. He also discovered, after injecting penicillin into a rabbit and a mouse, that penicillin did not produce any bad effects in a healthy animal.

One day, a member of the St. Mary's rifle team developed an eye infection. By this time, Fleming's helpers had developed a partially purified form of penicillin. Fleming believed the drug was safe to use on his friend's eye. With the man's consent, Fleming treated the infected eye with penicillin. The infection cleared up almost instantly.

Fleming was more and more certain that he had found a safe substance with great bacteria-fighting potential. But, in the course of investigating what penicillin could do, he and his co-workers also made some important discoveries about what it could not do. For instance, penicillin did not affect the germs that cause influenza, whooping cough, acne, or the common cold. Because of this, Fleming decided to promote penicillin as a reagent—a substance that shows the presence of something else by process of elimination.

Used in this way, penicillin proved particularly useful in helping researchers find and identify one of the microbes that was believed to cause influenza and other respiratory infections—Pfeiffer's bacillus. Doctors wanted to use the bacillus to make vaccines to fight such infections. But the microbe was difficult for doctors to locate and grow. On throat cultures taken from sick people, Pfeiffer's bacillus was often overgrown by other germs, making it impossible to identify and isolate.

Fleming hit upon the idea of using penicillin—which affected many or most of the other germs apt to be present on a throat swab from a patient, but did not affect Pfeiffer's bacillus—to separate Pfeiffer's from the other microbes. In what became a routine laboratory test, penicillin was introduced into a culture from a sick person. The penicillin soon slowed or stopped the growth of most of the germs in the culture. Pfeiffer's bacillus, if present, kept growing, along with just a few other germs. Researchers could now examine the culture, isolate Pfeiffer's bacillus, and allow it to continue growing until they had enough Pfeiffer's bacteria to make a vaccine.

The reagent use of penicillin was the subject of a speech Fleming gave to the Medical Research Club in February 1929. Facing a familiar audience, Fleming explained how penicillin could be used to isolate and identify germs such as Pfeiffer's bacillus. And then he went on to discuss the possibility of using penicillin as an antibacterial agent. However, Fleming's speaking skills had not improved since his speech on lysozyme. Fleming's words lacked passion and enthusiasm, and his presentation fell flat.

When he finished speaking, Fleming waited for comments or questions. He waited patiently, but in vain. No one had anything to say. Fleming's mind may have gone back to another moment seven years earlier, when he had presented his findings on lysozyme to this same group. Fleming had received the same reception then—absolutely no response at all. Alexander Fleming never forgot what he later referred to as "that frightful moment."

A few months later, in June 1929, a professional journal published a report by Fleming on penicillin. The report described penicillin as a "powerful antibacterial substance" that was non-toxic and non-irritating to animals. The conclusion read that the drug "may be an efficient antiseptic for application to, or injection into, areas infected with penicillin-sensitive microbes."

Fleming's paper would eventually have far-reaching significance. By the time it was published, however, Fleming's intense six-month involvement with penicillin had ended.

Over the next ten years, Fleming did not forget about penicillin. He mentioned penicillin's possibilities to other researchers. He continued to culture the penicillin mold in containers of broth, and he supplied mold juice samples to bacteriologists in other labs. But Fleming himself did not continue to test penicillin.

Why did Fleming stop his work on penicillin in 1929? He had seen how effective penicillin was in eliminating harmful bacteria in petri dishes. He had injected the drug into healthy animals without harming them. Why, then, didn't Fleming take the next crucial step and inject penicillin into an infected animal to see whether the animal could be cured? No one really knows. But if we look at the circumstances of Fleming's work, we can suggest some answers to these questions.

First, Fleming may have had good reason to doubt penicillin's effectiveness within a live body. Early tests showed that it took about four hours for penicillin to kill bacteria. Other tests showed that penicillin lost its bacteria-fighting power in the blood in about half an hour. The researchers working with Fleming were not able to concentrate penicillin, or to stabilize the drug, to keep it from losing its strength so rapidly. Fleming may have reasoned that there would not be time for penicillin to kill the harmful bacteria before the drug lost its strength.

Second, Fleming may have been influenced by Sir Almroth Wright. Wright, along with many other people, doubted that systemic cures, cures in which a medicine was introduced into the body to kill harmful bacteria throughout the body, could work. His own interest still lay almost entirely in vaccines to encourage the body to build up its own defenses against a disease. He remained confident that vaccine therapy eventually would be used for cures, as well as for prevention. Wright's beliefs may have kept Fleming from pressing his superior for funds and time to proceed with the testing of penicillin.

Third, perhaps Fleming remembered the years he had spent working with lysozyme, a substance that had not repaid its promise as a useful systemic antibiotic. Perhaps he began to suspect that what some colleagues were telling him was true: like lysozyme, penicillin was a waste of time.

Whatever the reasons, most of Fleming's work on penicillin had ended by mid-1929. For the next twelve years, penicillin was used primarily to isolate Pfeiffer's bacillus for making vaccines to protect against influenza. This routine use at St. Mary's, and in other labs, served to keep the penicillin mold alive and available. When the mold was finally studied seriously again, and then developed into the antibiotic that revolutionized medicine and saved millions of lives, the research was not done by Alexander Fleming, but by scientists in a lab about fifty miles away from St. Mary's.

6

The Makings of a Miracle

After his 1929 paper on penicillin, Alexander Fleming continued to stress penicillin's importance in isolating germs, such as Pfeiffer's bacillus, in cultures. Fleming's lab notebooks, papers, and speeches show that, between 1929 and 1931, he conducted some scattered experiments on penicillin as a local antiseptic. But, penicillin no longer dominated Fleming's work.

Fleming's most important continuing responsibility was supervising the production of vaccines for use at St. Mary's Hospital and for sale. This work could not be neglected, for vaccine sales funded the bulk of the Inoculation Department's research program. In 1932, he received an honor that showed how highly Fleming was regarded in the medical research community: he was elected President of the Section of Pathology of the Royal Society of Medicine, the most respected, influential, and exclusive scientific society in the world.

Then, in the mid-1930s, Fleming began new and challenging laboratory research on a group of medicines called the sulpha drugs. Like salvarsan, the sulpha drugs were laboratory-made combinations of chemicals. Unlike salvarsan, which seemed to cure only syphilis, the sulpha drugs were effective against many serious infections, including pneumonia, scarlet fever, and meningitis. From his own research, and the research of other scientists, Fleming learned that the sulpha drugs did not actually kill bacteria, but merely weakened them and stopped their growth. He reasoned that, after the bacteria had been weakened, the body's own germ-fighting cells took over to kill the now helpless microbes. Fleming became interested in combining vaccine therapy with sulpha drug treatment. He hoped that the vaccines would strengthen the body's ability to kill the bacteria, while the sulpha drugs weakened the bacteria and inhibited their growth. The sulpha drugs served as the focus of Fleming's research for many years, and he published several papers on the combined use of vaccines, and of chemicals, in fighting illnesses.

Personal events also occupied Alexander during this time. In 1935, his brother John became seriously ill with pneumonia. Fortunately, the pneumonia responded to treatment, and John was cured. Two years later, however, John suffered a second attack of pneumonia. This time John did not recover, and he died in 1937. The whole Alexander Fleming family keenly felt the loss. The brothers had been good friends, and

John and his wife, Sarah's twin sister, were frequent visitors at Alexander and Sarah's country home.

In 1938, the family circle grew smaller when fourteen-year-old Robert left home to attend boarding school. Alexander and Sarah missed their son greatly. Now they saw him only on occasional visits to the school, and during vacations.

That same year, 1938, brought great changes to Europe. In March, Hitler's Nazi Germany took over Austria. Later that year, Hitler demanded the Sudetenland, a part of Czechoslovakia. Britain and France, hoping to avoid another world war, agreed to let Hitler have his way. But, then, Germany occupied all of Czechoslovakia, and a few months later the Nazis invaded Poland. The British and French could no longer stand back and let Hitler conquer Europe. In September 1939, both countries declared war on Germany. World War II had begun.

Alexander and Sarah Fleming were in the United States when England declared war. Alec had delivered a paper at the Third International Congress of Microbiology, in New York City, on the advantage of combining vaccine therapy and chemical therapy, or chemotherapy, with sulpha drugs. The couple hurriedly sailed home. In England, Fleming's skills in developing and injecting vaccines, as well as the skills he had acquired during World War I, in treating wounds, were soon in great demand.

In late August of 1940, Fleming picked up a copy of the British medical journal *Lancet*. An article in the journal stated that researchers at Oxford University, just a short train ride from Fleming's lab in London, were testing penicillin. Fleming read that the researchers had tested penicillin on diseased mice, and with great success.

The researcher directing the study at Oxford was Howard Florey, an Australian pathologist—a scientist who studies disease. Fleming and Florey had recently been in contact about lysozyme. Working closely with Florey was Ernst Chain, a Jew who had fled Hitler's Nazi Germany. Chain, a skilled biochemist, had finally succeeded in doing what Fleming and his research assistants had not been able to do: bringing Fleming's mold juice to a usable condition—purer, concentrated, and stable.

The Oxford team had begun their work on penicillin in 1938. A year earlier, Florey and Chain, both interested in natural antibacterial agents, had succeeded in purifying Fleming's lysozyme. Then they had begun looking for a new antibacterial substance to test. They had examined several hundred papers and reports. Eventually, Fleming's 1929 paper on penicillin attracted their attention, and they decided to investigate the drug further. Florey and Chain did not need to ask Fleming for a mold sample, because a laboratory at Oxford University had a culture of the very penicillin mold that had landed in Fleming's petri dish twelve years earlier.

In September 1939, Florey had applied to the British Medical Research Council for funds to study penicillin. This organization approved, funded, and oversaw scientific research in England. Florey hoped to develop a pure form of penicillin that could be injected into a living body so that he could study how the drug fought infection. In his application, Florey listed some common infectious germs against which penicillin had proved effective. He observed that the drug might "possibly be of great practical importance."

However, with the nation gearing up for war, the Medical Research Council had little interest in funding research on unknown drugs. But Florey was determined. He tried a new tactic, appealing for money to a research center in the United States, which had not yet entered the war. Florey sent a proposal to the Rockefeller Foundation, a major center for medical research, in New York City. Evidently impressed by Florey's proposal, the Foundation agreed to fund his work on penicillin for five years—two more years than Florey had asked for.

Once Florey had acquired the necessary funds, Chain was able to work on his first major goal: obtaining an extract of penicillin pure enough to be safely injected into a living body. By March 1940, Chain developed a more purified form of the drug than Fleming ever had. Chain promptly repeated the testing Fleming had done on healthy animals: first on two mice, and then on more. Although the purer penicillin extract was much stronger than Fleming's mold juice, all the animals came through the tests unharmed.

Florey and Chain were eager to proceed with their next tests, tests that Fleming had never attempted, administering the drug to sick animals. But

Chain had not yet been able to concentrate the drug to produce a stronger dosage, or to stabilize the substance so that it would not lose strength so quickly. To solve the problem of penicillin taking longer to fight bacteria than the drug itself remained in the blood, Florey and Chain decided simply to give the animals repeated shots.

The first tests were done on small groups of mice that had been infected with a deadly disease known to respond to penicillin. Howard Florey and another chemist, Norman Heatley, took turns treating half the mice for one day and one night. The remainder of the mice, those in the "control" group, were not treated with any penicillin. By the next morning, all the control mice were dead. But the mice that had received penicillin therapy for twenty-four hours were still alive.

The Oxford team was encouraged. Chain referred to the test results as a miracle, and Florey began to plan and conduct more experiments.

As the Florey team proceeded methodically through the stages of developing and testing penicillin, German armies were taking over the European continent. By mid-1940, Britain was the only western European country at war with Germany that had not been invaded and defeated by Hitler's armies. Because Britain is an island country, separated from the European continent by water, Hitler's forces could attack the British only by sea or by air. Grimly, the British prepared themselves for a massive air attack.

Like many other British citizens, Florey and his

colleagues took turns leaving work to dig trenches and air-raid shelters for protection against German bombs. They also took steps to safeguard the penicillin mold. To make sure the mold would not be destroyed in the bombing, they smeared penicillin into the linings of their jackets. If the lab was destroyed, they hoped one of them might escape with enough penicillin spores to grow the mold again.

Despite the difficulties created by the war, Florey's research group finally managed to produce enough penicillin for a large-scale test. They infected fifty white mice with deadly streptococci, bacteria that can cause strep throat or scarlet fever in humans. Within a day, all twenty-five control mice were dead. However, of the twenty-five mice treated with penicillin for two days, twenty-four were cured. It was this experiment that was described in the *Lancet* issue Alexander Fleming saw.

When Fleming read the article, he called Florey and made an appointment to visit the laboratory at Oxford. Fleming arrived at the Oxford research center almost twelve years to the day after he had first discovered the blue mold. He thoroughly examined the Oxford team's research. He had few questions or comments but simply told Chain, "You have made something of my substance." Chain later recalled the visit: "He [Fleming] struck me as a man who had difficulty in expressing himself, though he gave the impression of being somebody with a very warm heart doing all he could to appear cold and distant."

Fleming seemed pleased by what he saw. He

later told friends the Oxford team had the chemists he had needed twelve years earlier. During Fleming's visit, Florey gave Fleming some of the concentrated penicillin the team had used. Fleming later tested its strength and decided that penicillin was a stronger antiseptic than the sulpha drugs.

At about this time, the Germans began an intense air war against Britain. As casualties mounted, Fleming was kept busy tending the wounded, both military and civilian. Many of the staff of St. Mary's moved to safer quarters outside London, but Alexander and Sarah did not leave. They agreed that Fleming should stay and treat the wounded in the wards of St. Mary's Hospital.

One evening in November 1940, the Flemings returned from dinner with friends to find their house had been set afire by bombs. Firemen were still fighting the flames. Alec and Sarah moved in with a friend until they were finally able to return to their home the following March. Less than a month later, a bomb exploded right next to the house, blowing in windows and doors and collapsing ceilings. The Flemings were asleep and lucky to escape with their lives.

While Fleming was occupied with the war, the Oxford team continued their efforts to develop penicillin. One of their greatest challenges was to accumulate a large enough quantity of the drug, so it could be tested on humans. Florey committed nearly all of his laboratory space and resources to growing penicillin. His team designed and made special equipment for growing the mold. Finally, as the doses were slowly produced, Florey began the crucial human tests, one by one.

The results of the initial tests on humans were mixed. One of the Oxford team's first patients was a police officer, who had developed an infection after a thorn from a rosebush scratched his face. The man was dying when Florey's team began injecting penicillin, but he began to improve after only twenty-four hours of treatment. The researchers gave him penicillin for another four days, and the man's condition continued to improve. Then, after the researchers had used penicillin injections to save the life of a boy dying of an infection after a hip operation, the policeman suffered a relapse. Unfortunately, the researchers had used all their penicillin in treating the boy. They watched helplessly as the man's condition worsened, and he finally died.

Florey was certain his team had a drug that worked, was safe, could save thousands of lives in the war, and might revolutionize medicine. But he urgently needed enough penicillin to conduct a program of careful testing that would convince the British authorities to lend greater support to his effort. He had to learn more about how the drug worked in humans.

Desperate for greater funding to produce penicillin in larger quantities, Florey and Heatley packed some of the mold into test tubes in June 1941, and flew to the United States, which was still not involved in the war. Florey traveled around the country for three months, trying to drum up interest in the "miraculous" curative qualities of his drug. Finally, he persuaded a government agency and a group of major U.S. drug companies to take on, jointly, the development of penicillin. He hoped that when they had solved the technical problems of producing the drug in quantity, they would send him the penicillin he needed to carry on his testing.

Florey then returned to Oxford, but Heatley remained in the United States, working with the U.S. Department of Agriculture to cultivate the penicillin mold on a large scale. Up to this time, all penicillin molds had come from the original blue mold Fleming had discovered in 1928. But researchers at the U.S. lab wanted to find and test other mold strains, just as Fleming had done when he began his investigations. The researchers hoped to find a strain of mold that could produce more penicillin than the original blue mold. Volunteers from the U.S. army collected and shipped molds to the lab from all over the world. A worker at the Department of Agriculture lab brought in so many samples of mold that she became known as Moldy Mary. One day, in 1943, Mary brought in a piece of rotting cantaloupe. Growing on the cantaloupe was a golden-colored mold, which turned out to produce more than twice the amount of penicillin produced by Fleming's blue mold. The scientists soon developed a sub-strain of this mold, which produced enough penicillin at low cost to make large-scale testing and treatment with penicillin practical.

Meanwhile, shortly after Florey had returned to Britain, the Japanese bombed Pearl Harbor on December 7, 1941, and the United States joined the war. Unfortunately for the Oxford team, America's entry into the war meant that the penicillin produced in America was kept for treatment of American battle casualties. As a result, Florey did not receive the large amounts of penicillin he had expected from the United States.

Instead, Florey and Chain were forced to step up production in their own lab, which was fast becoming a penicillin factory. By 1942, the Oxford team had enough penicillin to conduct further trials on human beings. The results were excellent. In one experiment, fifteen patients, each suffering from a serious infection that ordinarily caused death, were treated with penicillin. Of the fifteen, only one died.

Then, in August of that same year, Alexander Fleming re-entered the penicillin scene. He had a friend who was very ill with an undiagnosed ailment, with symptoms similar to those of meningitis. The man had not responded to any treatments and was close to death, when Fleming identified the microbe causing the illness and found it was one that responded to penicillin. Fleming telephoned Florey to ask for enough penicillin to treat his friend. Florey agreed immediately. According to some accounts, Florey himself took the train to St. Mary's to deliver the penicillin, along with instructions on how to use it. A month later, Fleming's friend was completely cured.

Fleming had now seen for himself how penicillin could reverse the course of a normally fatal illness, and he was impressed. He went to the British authorities to argue the importance of developing the drug. As a result of his and Florey's campaigning, a group of British drug companies finally organized to work on developing penicillin quickly and in great quantity.

In March 1943, Florey and his wife, Dr. Ethel Florey, who had directed the penicillin tests on human beings, published an article summarizing the successful results of penicillin testing. The Floreys warned readers not to come to them for the drug yet, as only the smallest quantities were available.

The Floreys did have enough penicillin to send some to British doctors tending wounded soldiers in North Africa, however. A doctor there later reported that he had used the drug on a young officer, who "had been in bed for six months with compound fractures in both legs." The young officer, said the doctor, "was little more than skin and bone and was running a high temperature. Normally he would have died in a very short while." A month after penicillin treatment was begun, the officer was on his feet. The doctor had enough penicillin to treat ten more cases, and nine of them were complete cures.

As stories about the miracle cures produced by penicillin began to make newspaper headlines, requests for the drug grew more urgent. And increased demand for penicillin created a serious controversy among the army medical staff. Field doctors noticed that a dose or two of penicillin produced a speedy cure for gonorrhea, a sexually-transmitted disease that was common among British soldiers in North Africa. Although gonorrhea is not life threat-

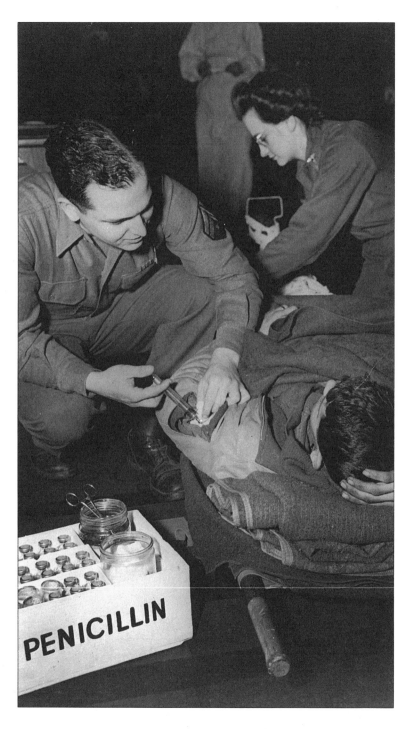

A soldier receiving penicillin during World War II

ening, it causes great discomfort, and about one third of the British army in North Africa was disabled by the disease.

The conflict was this: Should doctors use the precious miracle drug to save the lives of wounded men, who had fought in their country's service? Or should doctors use their limited stores of penicillin to cure men whose lives were not in danger, so these soldiers would be well enough to fight? The medical authorities decided that, since military advantage was best served by having more soldiers able to fight, the penicillin should be used to treat gonorrhea.

Fortunately, shortly after this conflict was resolved, the quantity of available penicillin increased tremendously, and fewer difficult choices had to be made about how best to use the drug. In the United States alone, the production of penicillin increased from enough to treat 170 cases in June 1943, to 40,000 cases in June 1944, to more than 250,000 cases in June 1945. By the time Germany was defeated in May 1945, penicillin was widely available and had already saved millions of lives.

7

All Mankind is in Their Debt

During World War II, penicillin was such an important lifesaving tool, that details about its production and effectiveness were kept secret. However, when the war ended in 1945, this secrecy was lifted, and the full story of the drug became public knowledge. Penicillin moved quickly into the mainstream of medical practice, and its use as a common treatment for infection revolutionized the care of the sick. Penicillin does not cure all diseases—sicknesses caused by viruses, for example, are untouched by the drug. And it cannot be used by everyone—some people are violently allergic to it. Even so, penicillin became, and remains today, one of a doctor's main tools in treating infection and disease.

Penicillin also changed the focus of medical research. Doctors began to concentrate less on creating immunity through the use of vaccines, and focused more on curing diseases.

In the years after World War II, the acclaim for Fleming's discovery, and for Fleming, grew and grew. By one biographer's count, Fleming was given, "25 honorary degrees, 26 medals, 18 prizes, 13 decorations, the freedoms of 15 cities and boroughs, and honorary membership in 89 academies and societies."

The Oxford team's contribution to the development of penicillin was also recognized, but at a much more modest level. A garden was dedicated to the researchers at Oxford University. The plaque there reads: "This rose garden was given in honour of the research workers in this university who discovered the clinical importance of penicillin. For saving of life, relief of suffering and inspiration to further research all mankind is in their debt."

Florey and Fleming both were knighted—given an honorary rank that entitled them to use the title "Sir" before their names. And the 1945 Nobel Prize for Physiology and Medicine was awarded to both Alexander Fleming and the Florey and Chain team, although the press coverage emphasized Fleming. There was no doubt that most of the world's admiration, praise, and thanks went to Fleming, who had concentrated on his mold juice for about seven months, rather than to the Oxford group, who had worked for more than five years to develop penicillin as an effective medical treatment.

Why was this so? Perhaps partly because Howard Florey seemed purposely to keep himself out of the limelight. He did not like the press and would barely speak with reporters. Besides, Florey had little time to entertain the public, or to grant interviews. He was still testing penicillin and teaching doctors how to use the drug.

Some people believe Fleming became the center of attention because his discovery of the mold was so dramatic and made such a good story. The work done by the Oxford group, on the other hand, involved less exciting, methodical trial-and-error refining of the drug and its testing and re-testing under different conditions. This work was much harder to understand, and did not make nearly as exciting a story. Also, while the work at Oxford was done by a group, the discovery was made by just one scientist.

Whatever the reason, the first attention came Fleming's way in August 1942, just after he had cured his friend with the then very rare penicillin given him by Florey. While what happened to Florey's patients never really became widely known, the recovery of Fleming's friend attracted great press notice. This "miracle cure" was the first the British public learned about the promising new antibiotic.

That same month, the *Times*, a leading newspaper in England, published an article urging quick development of penicillin. The article mentioned neither Fleming nor Florey. A few days later, Sir Almroth Wright wrote a letter to the *Times*, suggesting that credit be given to Fleming, both as the discoverer of penicillin and as the first to suggest its important medical applications. After Wright's letter was printed, public excitement about the new drug focused on Fleming. People became fascinated with Fleming's story of the discovery of penicillin. Alexander Fleming at first "deplored" all the personal fuss, or so he wrote to Florey. Years later, Fleming said in a speech, "When penicillin became a newspaper item my quiet existence was shattered. I had to learn how to cope with reporters; I had to make speeches; I had to learn how to broadcast."

However, the man who had once had a reputation for giving dull speeches learned very quickly how to charm the public and the press. He rarely denied any reporter an interview, and he accepted numerous public-speaking invitations. Perhaps, at first, Fleming felt he had to cooperate, for the publicity was certainly good for the Inoculation Department. But, after a while, Fleming no doubt began to enjoy the attention.

Sarah Fleming was proud of her husband and delighted in his fame. She often accompanied him to banquets and receptions in England, and on speaking tours in the United States and other countries. Gradually, however, her health began to deteriorate. During a June 1948 visit to Spain, Sarah fell ill, and had to spend most of her time confined to her bed in her hotel room. After this, she stopped going with Alexander to the ceremonies and dinners that occupied so much of his time, and she no longer traveled with him. Although nobody seemed to know exactly why Sarah's health was slowly failing, a colleague of Alexander's described her illness as "a painful disease of the spine that was quite incurable, and which also affected her mind."

Although Fleming was very distressed about Sarah's worsening condition, he dutifully continued his schedule of public appearances and tours. In his speeches, Fleming often stressed the role that chance had played in his life. "It may be said that I have achieved success," he once said. "I suppose I have, but in my success, as in the success of many others, fate or destiny, fortune or chance, call it what you will, has had a good deal to do."

Fleming believed it was chance that led him to become a medical student, chance that directed him to the Inoculation Department at St. Mary's, and, very obviously, chance that led him to the discovery of penicillin. "If the wrong mould had contaminated a culture of the right bacteria nothing extraordinary would have been seen," he once explained. "If the right mould had contaminated a culture of the wrong bacteria nothing extraordinary would have been seen. Even if the right mould had contaminated a culture of the right bacteria at the wrong time nothing extraordinary would have been seen. Further than that, if my mind when I saw it, had been occupied with other things I would have missed it. I might have been too busy to bother about chance happenings."

When Alexander Fleming wasn't traveling, receiving honors, making speeches, or giving interviews, his work, for the most part, proceeded as it had before he became so famous. In 1946, Sir Almroth Wright retired as head of the St. Mary's Institute of

Pathology and Director of the Inoculation Department. Fleming succeeded Wright, but he made very few changes in the lab.

Fleming's personal life also remained largely unchanged until the death of his wife in October 1949, after thirty-four years of marriage. Sarah's death left him alone—and lonely—in their big London home. The Flemings' son, Robert, was busy studying medicine at St. Mary's Hospital Medical School, as his father had before him. Fleming spent most of his free time with his friends at the club, or with his brother Robert's family.

Several years after Sarah's death, Fleming fell in love with a researcher at his lab. Dr. Amalia Voureka was an attractive Greek widow, and she shared Alexander's love of medicine. They married in April 1953, when Alexander was seventy-one years old, and together they enjoyed a very busy work and social life.

Every weekday morning, Alec and Amalia went together to work at the St. Mary's lab. After work, Alec usually drove Amalia home, before he went to his club. He played games at the club until seven o'clock; then he went home to change his clothes for his and Amalia's evening engagement. The couple rarely spent quiet evenings alone. Usually they went out for dinner or entertained guests in their home. Amalia was often impressed by Alexander's tireless energy.

In January 1955, Alexander Fleming, then

Fleming and Amalia Voureka on their wedding day

seventy-seven years old, retired as administrator of the St. Mary's Institute. He had never much liked administrative duties, and he wanted to devote more time to laboratory research. Unfortunately, that March, just a few months after his retirement, Fleming was stricken with a massive heart attack. He died at home, suddenly, unexpectedly.

The public was greatly saddened by the loss of one of the most beloved healers of all time. The *British Medical Journal* summed up Fleming's great achievement: "It is natural that the world will acclaim a medical advance 'great' in proportion to the curative benefits it brings, and on this count alone Sir Alexander Fleming has his place among the immortals. And close beside him will be Sir Howard Florey and Dr. Ernst Chain, who in a systematic investigation of antibacterial substances ten years later hit upon the technical ways and means of fulfilling the promise Fleming held out for penicillin in 1929. Fleming had the real naturalist's capacity for observation and the scientific imagination to see the implication of the observed fact—a capacity and an imagination which, it is true, only the prepared mind can compass, and which in the great discovery seem invariably to be joined to a mind that is essentially humble."

Publications around the world printed tributes to Alexander Fleming after his death, and many memorials were created in his honor. Medical centers and research institutes were named after him. Even a crater on the moon was named in honor of the beloved "father" of penicillin.

* * *

Was it fair that Alexander Fleming, who discovered penicillin by accident, received most of the credit for the drug? Perhaps, rather than debating fairness, it is important to recognize that there are many parts to be played in the complex process of bringing a new drug into use, and that some people are more suited to one role in that process than to another.

Fleming played with microbes, and he was a searcher and an observer. His appreciation of nature as a child, his experience with lysozyme, and his desire to discover a germ-fighting substance, all had prepared him to recognize the possible importance of the penicillin mold. A less experienced, less knowledgeable scientist probably never would have known enough to preserve the mold. "I have no doubt that the same phenomenon had been presented by accident to other bacteriologists," Fleming once said, "but they were not interested and so the chance was missed."

Sir Howard Florey had equally important skills, but of a different kind. A fine scientist, he recognized the potential value of penicillin in treating and curing diseases. He also had the leadership ability needed to assemble a team to refine penicillin. And he had the drive and determination to find the money needed to perform tests on the drug, and to begin to produce penicillin in quantities large enough to be useful in treatment.

Although Fleming never said so, the question of

why someone else completed the work on his discovery seemed to disturb him. Once, the head of a large chemical company asked Fleming why he himself had not developed penicillin as a cure. Why had he left it to the Oxford group to develop its enormous potential in treating bacterial infections? "Why didn't you [develop penicillin]?" Fleming snapped. "You had all the data and all the facilities."

As the years passed, Fleming refined his explanation of his own role in the development of the miracle drug. Four years before his death, in a speech at the University of Edinburgh, Scotland, he said, "My important part in the story was that I saw something unusual and appreciated something of its importance so that I set to work on it." In that same speech, Fleming also stressed that, while teamwork was crucial to developing a substance, so was the individual, for it was the individual who discovered.

"As the world becomes more complicated, so we are less and less able to carry through anything to a successful conclusion without the collaboration of others," Fleming said. "We are becoming too specialized for any one individual to have the knowledge of all the by-ways into which any problem leads us so we must have help. We make up a team. But by that I do not wish to decry the lone worker. It is the lone worker who makes the first advance in a subject, the details may be worked out by a team but the prime idea is due to the enterprise, thought or perception of an individual."

Alexander Fleming was the lone worker in the penicillin story. He made the first advance: discovery and careful preservation of the penicillin mold. Thanks to his contribution, the Florey research team was able to develop penicillin into a miracle drug that has benefited all mankind.

For Further Reading

Readers who want to know more about the life of Alexander Fleming and the discovery of penicillin may be interested in the following:

- *Alexander Fleming* by Richard Tames (Watts, Lifetimes series, 1990).
- *Breakthrough: The True Story of Penicillin* by Francine Jacobs (Putnam, 1985).
- *The Disease Fighters: The Nobel Prize in Medicine* by Nathan Aaseng. Discusses Fleming, Florey and Chain in a chapter titled "Magic Bullets" (Lerner, 1987).
- *Portraits of Nobel Laureates in Medicine and Physiology* by Sarah R. Riedman and Elton T. Gustafson. Covers the work of Fleming, Florey and Chain in a chapter titled "Green Mold in the Breeze" (Abelard-Schuman, 1963).
- *Nobel Prize Winners* edited by Frank N. Magill (Magill Books/Salem Press, 1989).

Index

References to photographs are listed in *italic,* **boldface** type.